Come, Let Us Adore Him!
An invitation to Adore Jesus in the Blessed Sacrament All Year Long.
Written by Martha Gómez Hinojosa
Illustrated by Daniela García

This book Belongs to:

____

To Jesus, Aaron and baby Daniel

"Let the children come to me, and do not prevent them;
for the kingdom of heaven belongs to such as these."

Matthew 19:14

All you children, come, let us adore Him!

His name is Jesus, and He is your friend.

He loves you so much that He gave
His own life for you and for many.

"Yes, you, with the big wide smile and your brown,
blue, green or hazel eyes."

He is waiting for you to come, to sing, pray, and bow before Him. He wants to give you many blessings.

All you have to do is to open your heart to Him.

All you children, come, let us adore Him.
Fall on your knees with your arms wide open.

Receive His love, His peace, and His joy.

Close your eyes and feel
His heavenly presence.

Imagine angels singing to Him and saints
kneeling down respectfully before Him.

Now take a deep breath, and as you inhale, imagine
you are smelling the sweet scent of roses from heaven.

Now exhale and release all your fears, worries, and anxieties. Picture them fading away into the air.
Worries
Fears

Keep breathing in that heavenly rose scent.

Because Jesus Himself is heaven, and His sweet aroma fills the celestial garden and your soul with serenity.

Open your eyes and imagine two beautiful
rays of light coming from the heart
of Jesus into your own heart.

Close your eyes again and feel the heart of Jesus beating in sync with your own.

As both hearts beat together, say to Him,
"Jesus, thank you for dying on the cross for me."

"Please forgive me if I haven't listened to my parents when they told me to pick up my toys and dirty clothes."

"Forgive me for not always being kind to my friends at school. I am sorry."

"Now, that you are in my heart, please stay with me always. With your help, I promise to do better. Jesus, I trust you."

Keep feeling His heart beating with yours
and say three times, "Jesus, I love you.
Jesus, I love you. Jesus, I love you."

Now, picture Him giving you a big hug and filling you with His love.

Imagine Him telling you, "Thank you for coming to spend time with Me, my child.
Sometimes I feel alone, but today you made Me feel very happy."

"Do you want to ask Me for something? I'm listening to you." Then you say to Him, "Yes my Jesus. I ask for peace in my house, in my city, in my country, and in the world."

Then with His hands, He touches your head and says to you,
"May peace always be with you. Wherever you go, it will go spread
out to the world with you."

Right after that, you feel the beautiful and strong power
of Jesus' peace, in your heart, mind, body, and soul.

Open your eyes, Holy Hour has come to an end. Let's all say goodbye to Jesus in the Blessed Sacrament. Blow Him a kiss and thank Him again in your heart for this precious time with Him.

But wait, before you go, He is giving
you a blessing, and you sing a song for
Him, "Holy God, we praise Thy name..."

And don't forget, next time, tell your friends,
"All you children, come, let us adore Him."
He's always waiting for you in the Blessed Sacrament.

When you adore Jesus in the Blessed Sacrament, you glorify
the Father, the Son, and the Holy Spirit in heaven. Amen.